IMAGES
of America

FORT LOGAN

Here is what a typical busy time at the Fort Logan Denver & Rio Grande Railroad depot looked like in 1918. With duffel bags in hand, individual troops board the train to go to their new assignments during World War I. (FHFLC.)

ON THE COVER: Fort Logan troops are shown in a review ceremony on the spacious parade ground around 1895. The headquarters building is in the background. (Courtesy of the Colorado Historical Society.)

IMAGES
of America

FORT LOGAN

Jack Stokes Ballard, PhD, and
the Friends of Historic Fort Logan

ARCADIA
PUBLISHING

Published by Arcadia Publishing
Charleston, South Carolina

Printed in the United States of America

Library of Congress Control Number: 2011926799

For all general information, please contact Arcadia Publishing:
Telephone 843-853-2070
Fax 843-853-0044
E-mail sales@arcadiapublishing.com
For customer service and orders:
Toll-Free 1-888-313-2665

Visit us on the Internet at www.arcadiapublishing.com

*This book is dedicated to all the men and women who
faithfully served, militarily and medically, at Fort Logan.*

CONTENTS

ACKNOWLEDGMENTS

A number of organizations provided photographs and historical material that collectively became the contents of this book and made this pictorial history of Fort Logan come alive. While the majority of the photographs come from the Friends of Historic Fort Logan Collection (herein noted as FHFLC), the Denver Public Library (DPL), Colorado Historical Society (CHS), Fort Laramie National Historic Site (FLNHS), Colorado Railroad Museum, Colorado Mental Health Institute at Fort Logan (CMHI-FL), and Fort Logan National Cemetery also made notable contributions. Their assistance has proven invaluable in telling the Fort Logan story.

In addition to organizations, a great number of individuals conscientiously labored to collect and select photographs, write captions, and organize all the historic material. The foundation for this book was laid many years ago by some farsighted people, organized as the Friends of Historic Fort Logan, who sought to establish a museum for the fort, preserve buildings, and begin archiving items. Foremost in that organization was Earl McCoy, a mental health center staff member, who became the longtime "historic memory of the Fort." More immediately, great thanks go to the Friends of Historic Fort Logan Board of Directors and, especially, the book committee, consisting of Jayne Howard, Judy Zelio, Margaret and Raymond Ziehm, Rebecca Watt, and William Leeper. They toiled long and hard and most gratefully moved the project to fruition. Others, such as staff members Kate Elder and Tony Raddell of the Colorado Mental Health Institute, Bonita Hutcheson of the Sheridan Historical Society, and O'Neal Hughes of the Fort Logan National Cemetery, provided valuable support in their respective areas. Throughout all the assembling of the book, the thoughtful and energetic guidance of Arcadia Publishing editor Debbie Seracini has been greatly appreciated.

INTRODUCTION

Fort Logan officially began on October 31, 1887, becoming an urban-type fort newly favored by the US Army. With reduced Indian troubles and a growing rail network, the Army had been considering ways to cut costs by closing scattered, isolated frontier posts, like Fort Laramie, Wyoming, and using the railroads to move troops throughout the West more efficiently and expeditiously.

This change in the Army's concept about Western forts coincided in 1886 with a desire by Denver business and civic leaders to boost their local economy by obtaining a nearby fort. This chamber of commerce promotion of Denver's strategic location with good rail connections led to Colorado senator Henry M. Teller introducing a bill that authorized the establishment of an Army post near Denver. Endorsed by the secretary of war, William Endicott, Congress passed the Teller bill, which President Cleveland signed on February 17, 1887. It appropriated $100,000 for construction with a required donation by state citizens of at least 640 acres.

Denver leaders impressively raised money to buy the required land and quickly proposed 11 sites in March 1887 for the Army chief of staff, Lt. Gen. Phil Sheridan, to visit and consider. Sheridan chose a relatively level, sagebrush-covered, treeless plateau about eight miles southwest of the city, bounded on the north by Bear Creek, on the east by the South Platte River Valley, and on the west by the mountains. One factor considered in the distance from Denver was to "keep away the saloons and other nuisances," or so the Army command hoped. By September, the purchase of the "Johnson Tract" occurred, and the first soldiers from the 18th Infantry arrived from posts in Kansas in October. Upon arrival, the troops mistakenly camped in 26 freezing tents on a nearby ranch but moved to the proper location on Halloween 1887, beginning what initially was called the "Camp Near the City of Denver." Maj. George K. Brady became the first commander.

Capt. Lafayette E. Campbell arrived in November to become quartermaster of the new fort and to supervise the building program. Permanent facility construction got underway in 1888 with brick officers' quarters (some duplexes), a headquarters, barracks for six infantry companies and four companies of cavalry, a commissary, a guardhouse, and other buildings, designed by architect Frank J. Grodavent, and arranged around a 32-acre parade ground. On July 1, 1888, the *Denver Republican* newspaper reported, "The Army Post will present a fine appearance, and will become one of the leading attractions and pleasure resorts of Denver." Also, in 1888, the Denver & Rio Grande Railroad built a spur line to the fort. Completion of the final building, which was to house bachelor officers in "Officers' Row," located around the parade ground, did not take place until 1897.

Citizens in the area referred to the new post as "Fort Sheridan," honoring the Civil War general who had selected the site. Sheridan, however, preferred having his name associated with a fort north of Chicago, so on April 5, 1889, the "Camp" officially became designated as Fort Logan, named for Civil War Union general and Illinois senator John Alexander Logan. Logan had achieved considerable fame for being commander of the Grand Army of the Republic and for a directive establishing May 30 as Decoration Day (the national celebration that later became Memorial Day). Also, Logan had visited Colorado and had invested in the state's mining. Unfortunately, he died in 1886 not knowing a fort was to be named after him.

The first infantry barracks were completed in May 1889, and Companies D and F of the 7th Infantry Regiment left Fort Laramie, then targeted for closure, for Fort Logan. They marched 206 miles arriving May 16. Two companies of the 18th Infantry, the initial units on the fort, moved into the permanent barracks. Col. Henry C. Merriam, the Fort Laramie 7th Infantry Regiment commander, arrived at Fort Logan on October 18, 1889, and became the commanding officer. He subsequently served for nearly eight years, which was longer than any other fort commander. The last of the 7th Infantry arrived by train in March 1890.

The first military action for Fort Logan troops occurred in December 1890 when Colonel Merriam and six companies deployed by train to Fort Sully, South Dakota, to intercept movement of Sioux tribal bands fleeing southward after Sitting Bull's death. The Fort Logan troops prevented some of the concentration of Sioux Ghost Dancers but did not participate in the culminating Wounded Knee Battle. Most Fort Logan troops returned in late January 1891, with the last elements arriving in February after a snowbound experience at Julesburg.

The year 1894 became very significant for a number of reasons. In March, five infantry companies moved by train to Denver Union Station "to have troops in readiness to quell anticipated riot, and to protect public property." This action resulted from Governor Waite's siege of the city hall and the threat of serious civil conflict. Later that same year, troops were ordered to Trinidad and New Castle, Colorado, and to Raton, New Mexico, to maintain peace and to protect property during the growing railroad labor strife. The Pullman rail strike had reached Colorado.

Also in 1894, Fort Logan became an Army Signal Corps observation balloon base. The hydrogen-inflated balloon, named the *General Myer*, transferred from Fort Riley, Kansas. A large wooden hangar was erected, and 28-year-old Sgt. Ivy Baldwin, a noted balloonist and aerialist, was recruited to operate the balloon. When a high wind destroyed the *General Myer*, Baldwin and his wife, Bertha, cut, sewed, fabricated, and varnished pongee silk to make a new balloon using the old basket and rigging. This balloon, along with Baldwin and support personnel, deployed to Santiago, Cuba, during the 1898 Spanish-American War. On the second day of ascensions during the battle, Spanish artillery punctured the already leaky balloon, thus ending ballooning at Fort Logan.

Additionally, in October 1894, the first cavalry unit, the 2nd Cavalry, came to Fort Logan from Fort Bowie, Arizona. Cavalry would remain at the post until 1904. Fort routine, the never-ending drill, marches, exercises, and classes, may have been boring for the men, but the dress parades, ceremonies, and athletic competitions attracted Denverites and nearby citizens. Cavalry units added to the attraction.

About 340 acres were added to the fort in 1908, which brought the reservation total to 980. Questions arose, however, whether to close or to expand the post. In September 1909, Fort Logan received a new designation as a "recruit depot," continuing that mission as a soldier induction center through World War I and until 1922. Some recruiting officers remained, however, and among the most notable was Maj. Dwight D. Eisenhower, who, with his wife, Mamie, lived in an officers' duplex next to the Field Officers' Quarters in 1924–1925.

In 1922, a company of the 38th Infantry was garrisoned at the fort, and a 2nd Engineer unit succeeded them in 1927. Improvements to the buildings and grounds came after the engineers took over the fort and during the 1930s Depression-era WPA money-and-workers-aided construction and rehabilitation. These improvements included new noncommissioned officers' duplexes on the eastern side. Also, during this period, Civilian Conservation Corps (CCC), Reserve Officers' Training Corps (ROTC), Citizens' Military Training Camps (CMTC), and other programs occupied some buildings.

As World War II loomed (1939), the 18th Engineer Brigade replaced the 2nd Engineer units, and early in 1941, the Army Air Corps established a clerk training sub-post of Lowry Field at Fort Logan. Hurried construction of wood-frame barracks and classrooms ensued, and the fort had an additional mission of serving as an Army induction center. In 1944, a convalescent hospital and a brief German prisoner of war camp came to Fort Logan with wartime personnel peaking at 5,500.

During the World War II demobilization, Fort Logan became a busy separation center, but with the decline of that requirement, the fort was declared surplus effective May 7, 1946. Some land and temporary wood-frame structures were then sold. About 580 acres were turned over to the Veterans Administration (VA), and it utilized the fort's hospital beds until the new Denver VA hospital opened in 1951.

State and federal officials advanced various postwar proposals for the future use of Fort Logan. However, with no set military requirement, Governor McNichols and the federal government reached agreement in December 1959 for a donation to the state of 308 acres. The state of Colorado took possession of land and buildings on April 1, 1960. At this same time, 75 acres were transferred to the Fort Logan National Cemetery, which had begun in 1889 as a small 3.2-acre post cemetery.

Colorado decided to use Fort Logan as a mental health center under the supervision of the Department of Institutions, and the first patients were admitted on July 17, 1961. Subsequently, in addition to new hospital buildings, many Fort structures were utilized for inpatient care, residential education, and treatment by various state human service agencies. In 1991, the center became the Colorado Mental Health Institute at Fort Logan. The parade ground remained as an open space primarily for youth soccer fields. The Field Officers' Quarters became a museum. If one listens carefully, the sounds of horses, drill, martial music, and colorful review ceremonies can still be heard at historical Fort Logan.

The Fort Logan Field Officers' Quarters (for rank of major or higher), with the children of an officer visible, is shown in this early photograph from around the 1890s. Currently, the volunteer organization Friends of Historic Fort Logan has worked to preserve and restore this building, developing it into a museum for the fort. This building, one of originally two on either side of the commanding officers' quarters, has become the focal point and logo of the Friends' efforts at preservation and education. (Courtesy of National Archives.)

One

Early Years
at Fort Logan

One of the earliest aerial photographs of Fort Logan, approximately 1895, was perhaps taken from the Fort Logan balloon. The view is looking west with six enlisted barracks and a large single barracks building in the foreground. In the background, the buildings belonging to Officers' Row can be seen in a semicircle around the large parade ground. Note the wide-open vistas that existed when the fort was first built. (FHFLC.)

Lt. Gen. Philip H. Sheridan, Army chief of staff, arrived in Denver by train on March 20, 1887, to consider 11 sites proposed by Denver citizens for the location of a new fort. Sheridan chose a level plateau site eight miles southwest of the city. Sheridan, a popular Union Civil War general, was nationally honored by this unusual "cigar card." (FHFLC.)

This photograph of General Sheridan did not provide the most flattering image, but his noted Civil War record and his selection of the site for Fort Logan led to the Sheridan name being adopted for the community that grew near the fort. Streets were also subsequently named Sheridan. (DPL.)

The unique layout of Fort Logan, at first called "Camp Near the City of Denver" and by some citizens "Fort Sheridan," had a looping half circle of buildings to the west around a very large central parade ground. Enlisted barracks anchored both ends of the horseshoe-like site plan. The headquarters or administration building, guardhouse, flagpole, and hospital formed the north side of the semicircle. (FHFLC.)

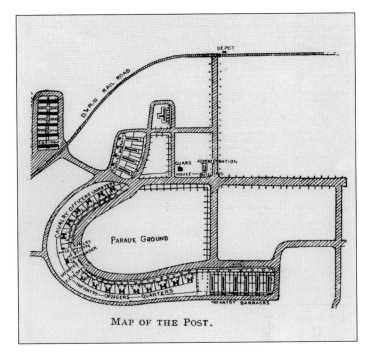

MAP OF THE POST.

Capt. Lafayette E. Campbell, shown here in civilian clothes, arrived at Fort Logan in November 1887 shortly after the first troops camped on the Fort Logan site on October 31, 1887, officially beginning the fort. Captain Campbell, as quartermaster, supervised construction of Fort Logan buildings. (FHFLC.)

13

Construction of red brick Fort Logan buildings began in 1888. By 1889, most of the permanent structures had been nearly completed, and troops and officers began moving into quarters that year. Workmen stand on the roof of a partially completed officers' duplex. (DPL.)

The Fort Logan contractor was Thomas H. O'Neill of Wichita, Kansas, and he recruited a large workforce both locally and from other states. (DPL.)

Frank J. Grodavent was the architect for the Fort Logan buildings. The large, multistory main buildings created an aura of permanence and stability that included architectural refinements. A Denver newspaper in 1888 declared, "The Army Post will present a fine appearance." This Grodavent photograph was taken November 13, 1887, at Leavenworth, Kansas. (FHFLC.)

This c. 1892 view of the officers' duplexes in the Officers' Row, located around the western side of the Fort Logan parade ground, represents one of the earliest photographs of fort buildings. Note the small trees. (Courtesy of National Archives.)

Here is another early c. 1892 photograph of Fort Logan's No. 17 officers' duplex. A pleasant day evidently allowed the families of officers to appear on the porches. An officer also stands at the duplex on the left. Newly planted trees are just starting to leaf out. (Courtesy of National Archives.)

Railroads were always important in respect to Fort Logan's location. As construction of the fort progressed in 1888, the Denver & Rio Grande Railroad built a spur line to the fort, and shortly thereafter, a handsome depot was added. This damaged photograph represents one of the very first depot scenes. Note the "Fort Logan" sign on the trackside. Later, a large sign appeared on the left side of the depot. (FHFLC.)

As Fort Logan buildings began to rise, a large building with a prominent tower could be seen easily in the treeless area on a hill directly north of the fort. This was the Loretto Heights Academy. This early postcard shows how the academy tended to dominate as a landmark in the area. (FHFLC.)

Loretto Heights Academy, Loretto, Colorado.

The Sisters of Loretto came to Denver in 1864 and established the Loretto Heights Academy and other schools, bringing Catholic education for girls to the territory and later to the state of Colorado. This postcard shows the imposing Loretto Heights Academy, which could be seen from Fort Logan and all the surrounding area. (FHFLC.)

B-4317

On April 5, 1889, Fort Logan was named after Union Civil War general John Alexander Logan. After the Civil War, General Logan became an Illinois senator and commanded the Grand Army of the Republic. He began the practice of decorating veteran graves, which later became Memorial Day. (Courtesy of National Archives.)

As Fort Laramie, Wyoming, began closing and enlisted barracks were completed at Fort Logan, the 7th Infantry Regiment began moving to Fort Logan. Companies D and F marched from Fort Laramie to Fort Logan, arriving in May 1889. A 7th Infantry Company stands at attention on the Fort Logan parade ground. Enlisted barracks can be seen in the background. (Merriam Album, courtesy of FLNHS.)

Col. Henry Clay Merriam commanded the 7th Infantry Regiment. He and his family, along with the headquarters staff and other regiment companies, arrived at Fort Logan by train on October 18, 1889. Colonel Merriam then began the longest tenure as fort commander, serving nearly eight years. (Courtesy of the Berger family collection.)

In this photograph, Col. Henry C. Merriam is shown seated at his desk in the Fort Logan headquarters building. He took pride in hosting visiting superior officers and in impressing them with his training program, especially marksmanship. (FHFLC.)

Colonel Merriam's wife, Una, pictured here, was born in Jamaica. After their marriage in June 1874, she experienced difficult pioneer conditions accompanying Colonel Merriam to primitive, isolated posts from the Rio Grande to the Pacific Northwest. (Courtesy of the Berger family collection.)

Colonel Merriam, his wife, Una, and their five children were the first occupants of the new commanding officers' quarters, shown here. The house stands approximately in the center of Officers' Row facing the parade ground. This building, the adjacent Field Officers' Quarters, and the rest of Officers' Row structures still exist today. (Merriam Album, courtesy of FLNHS.)

Colonel Merriam was the first fort commander to operate from this new headquarters building. Merriam had a reputation for being a strict, but fair, disciplinarian and always emphasized drill and marksmanship in his units. (Merriam Album, courtesy of FLNHS.)

In December 1890, only a relatively short time after Colonel Merriam and companies of the 7th Infantry Regiment had settled at Fort Logan, they were deployed by train to South Dakota to participate in a campaign against the Sioux Indians. Colonel Merriam, seated center, and 7th Infantry officers were photographed at Fort Sully, South Dakota. (Courtesy of National Archives.)

Headquarters tents of the 7th Infantry are shown in a camp near the forks of the Cheyenne River, South Dakota, in 1890. The troops did not participate in the Wounded Knee Battle but did intercept some Sioux bands moving south after Sitting Bull's death. (Courtesy of National Archives.)

The 2nd Cavalry came to Fort Logan from Fort Bowie, Arizona, on October 20, 1894. The original Fort Logan plan had anticipated assignment of up to four companies of cavalry. Cavalry units would remain at Fort Logan until 1904. Here, B Company of the 2nd Cavalry crosses the railroad tracks into Sedalia, Colorado, a few miles south of Fort Logan. (FHFLC.)

Cavalry stables, planned in the original fort concept, were built to the northwest and behind the Officers' Row buildings. No more than two cavalry companies were ever stationed at Fort Logan. (FHFLC.)

REGULARS BIVOUACKED AT THE DEPOT.

This drawing for a newspaper, based on a photograph by noted Denver photographer Harry H. Buckwalter, shows Fort Logan soldiers at Denver's Union Station on March 16, 1894. Colorado governor Davis H. Waite requested federal troops from the fort to act as a reserve force in his siege of fire and police board members barricaded in the city hall. The threat of serious violence fortunately eased, and the companies returned to Fort Logan. (FHFLC.)

In 1894, an Army Signal Corps balloon was transferred from Fort Riley, Kansas, to Fort Logan. A large hangar, to the west of Officers' Row, was constructed to house the balloon. The Army's war balloons were primarily used for observation of enemy forces and artillery spotting. (Courtesy of National Archives.)

24

In addition to the large observation balloon, the Fort Logan Army Signal Corps unit had responsibility for weather balloons, as seen here. The foothills can be viewed clearly in the background. This 1890s photograph is from the Signal Corps Collection. (Courtesy of National Archives.)

This 1897 photograph of the Fort Logan balloon shows it leaving the hangar and making an ascension. The Army recruited Ivy Baldwin, an experienced balloonist and aerial performer (probably standing in the basket), to make balloon ascensions and to manage balloon operations. They made him a sergeant. (Courtesy of National Archives.)

608. Eldorado Springs, Colo. Ivy Baldwin on the Tight Rope.
Height, 582 feet. Length, 530 feet.

Ivy Baldwin also became famous in the area for performances in balloons and other feats, such as tightrope walking, seen in this postcard. After the first Fort Logan balloon was destroyed in a high wind, Ivy Baldwin and his wife, Bertha, cut, sewed, and fabricated a new one out of pongee silk and then coated it with varnish. They used the rigging and basket from the old one to allow Fort Logan ballooning to continue. (FHFLC.)

In 1898, when the Spanish-American War began, Fort Logan's 7th Infantry Regiment and the balloon were deployed to war fronts in the Philippines and Cuba. The ship *Logan* transported men and equipment to the Philippines. In this scene, it is carrying members of the 14th Cavalry.

Sgt. Ivy Baldwin and the Fort Logan observation balloon went to Tampa, Florida, for transport to Cuba. Due to exposure to sun and heat, the balloon's fabric weakened and began leaking. Nevertheless, it made several ascensions at the battle for Santiago. This photograph shows the balloon in the attack on San Juan Hill. Spanish artillery punctured the balloon on the second day of ascensions, thereby ending Fort Logan ballooning. (Courtesy of National Archives.)

Shown during the 1890s, Col. Henry C. Merriam leads his immediate 7th Infantry officers and the regimental band in a Fort Logan parade. Merriam encouraged Denverites to come to the fort to witness such ceremonies. Enlisted barracks can be seen in the background. (Merriam Album, courtesy of FLNFS.)

The officers of the 7th Infantry Regiment are grouped by a Fort Logan building for this photograph. Some of the lieutenants and captains pictured would eventually rise to become general officers. This photograph, dated approximately 1897, was included in an album given to Colonel Merriam, probably as a going-away gift when he departed Fort Logan. (Merriam Album, courtesy FLNHS.)

Colonel Merriam leads his mounted officers in a dress parade at Fort Logan. Some observers in horse-drawn carriages can be spotted in the background. (Merriam Album, courtesy of FLNHS.)

One of the first buildings to be completed at Fort Logan was the guardhouse. It had a prominent location next to the flagpole and near the headquarters building. Note the soldiers sitting on the side of the guardhouse and the artillery pieces that came with the 7th Infantry from Fort Laramie. (Merriam Album, courtesy of FLNHS.)

Armed 7th Infantry troops pass in review in winter overcoats on the Fort Logan parade ground. (Merriam Album, courtesy of FLNHS.)

In 1897, the building for the bachelor officers' quarters was completed, becoming the last major structure to be built in the Fort Logan Officers' Row. It had a ballroom, and it sometimes served as an officers' club for social events. (Merriam Album, courtesy of FLNHS.)

Another grouping of the 7th Infantry officers at Fort Logan was photographed most likely in 1897. Colonel Merriam, regimental commander, is shown fourth from left in the seated row. (Merriam Album, courtesy of FLNHS.)

The 7th Infantry Band stands at attention awaiting orders to proceed as part of an elaborate pass-in-review ceremony on the parade ground. Besides military parades and ceremonies, the band would offer concerts on the post and in various communities. (Merriam Album, courtesy of FLNHS.)

Colonel Merriam was an excellent horseman dating from the days of the Civil War. Pictured, he leads a full-dress parade and ceremony mounted on his horse. (Merriam Album, courtesy of FLNHS.)

Officers of the 7th Infantry are shown with Colonel Merriam seated in the center. The officers in full military dress likely posed for this photograph following their parade ground ceremony. Merriam's Civil War Medal of Honor can be seen in the center of his uniform blouse, near the neck. Merriam was awarded the Medal of Honor for his role in the Battle of Fort Blakeley in 1865. (Merriam Album, courtesy of FLNHS.)

Fort Logan band concerts, as seen here, were held in the bandstand on the western edge of the parade ground and across from the commanding officers' quarters. As a public relations gesture, Fort Logan commanders, Colonel Merriam in particular, encouraged citizens to spend a Saturday afternoon at the fort for pleasant entertainment. (Merriam Album, courtesy of FLNHS.)

Company H of the 7th Infantry served at Fort Logan until April 20, 1898. The company drills with rifles on the spacious Fort Logan parade ground. (Merriam Album, courtesy of FLNHS.)

One of Colonel Merriam's key 7th Infantry officers was Lt. Col. Andrew S. Burt. He had been with Merriam at Fort Laramie. Later, as a colonel, he would become commander of the 25th Infantry Regiment and commander of Fort Logan from December 31, 1898, to June 19, 1899. (FHFLC.)

Troop routine at Fort Logan in 1898 usually began early in the day. Company enlisted men do "setting up exercises" after reveille. Barely visible in the left background is the Loretto Heights Academy Building. (FHFLC.)

The 25th Infantry Regiment, a black unit, served at Fort Logan from October 3, 1898, to June 27, 1899. Company G of the 25th was at Fort Logan from July 21, 1900, to September 22, 1900. This photograph from October 1898 shows the African American troops in a civic parade. (FHFLC.)

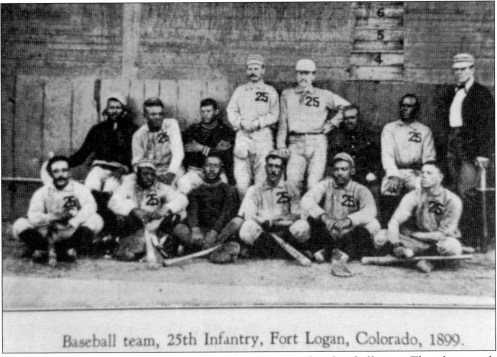

Baseball team, 25th Infantry, Fort Logan, Colorado, 1899.

The 25th Infantry Regiment was also noted for an outstanding baseball team. This photograph shows the 1899 players. (FHFLC.)

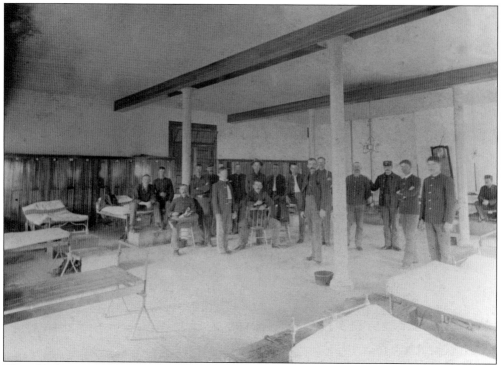

This old photograph provides an interior view of one of the Fort Logan enlisted barracks in the late 1890s. The men are attentive to the camera but otherwise quite relaxed. (FHFLC.)

DINING ROOM.

An obvious patriotic celebration is in store for an enlisted men's meal in a mess hall of one of the Fort Logan enlisted barracks. (FHFLC.)

Fort Logan's military families generally enjoyed being at the new urban-type fort. A young officer with a big smile proudly holds one of his children. (FHFLC.)

An officer's wife holds a child on a Fort Logan officers' duplex porch. Note the folding chair, which was designed for easy transporting in the many Army relocations. (FHFLC.)

A group of Fort Logan enlisted men is pictured in typical workday uniforms in the late 1890s. (FHFLC.)

After the Spanish-American War in 1898, Company D of the 7th Infantry returned to Fort Logan for a brief time. As the 1900s began, the 23rd Infantry and the 14th Cavalry manned the fort. Troops returned to the fort parade ground for drill and ceremonies. (FHFLC.)

Two

EARLY 1900S AND WORLD WAR I

Between 1894 and 1909, Fort Logan was base camp for eight different regiments of infantry and companies of four different cavalry regiments. In this photograph, Troop H, 14th Cavalry, leaves the Fort Logan stables area on September 27, 1902. Two stables appear on the right, and stores buildings are on the left. (FHFLC.)

This panoramic photograph from September 1902 shows stores and maintenance buildings at Fort Logan to the northwest of the Officers' Row and parade ground. (FHFLC.)

Fort Logan stables are pictured here. Stables were included in the original Fort plans, although cavalry units did not arrive until 1894. (FHFLC.)

John Hill was a trooper in Company H, 14th Cavalry, at Fort Logan (1901–1903). He is shown in front of a fort building, probably his barracks, in the cavalry dress uniform complete with gauntlets and saber. (FHFLC.)

This is another photograph of 14th Cavalry trooper John Hill. Here, he appears mounted on his horse with saber and full trail equipment. (FHFLC.)

Col. Francis A. Mansfield, commander of the 2nd Infantry (1904–1906) at Fort Logan, presents medals to members of the regiment on the parade ground. The headquarters, barracks, and firehouse buildings can be seen in the background. (FHFLC.)

Soldiers of Fort Logan's 2nd Infantry stand ready for a Saturday inspection. This photograph is dated 1904. (FHFLC.)

In 1905, Company L of the 2nd Infantry, depicted in heavy marching order, begin breaking ranks following a Saturday inspection. (FHFLC.)

A 2nd Infantry Company is shown training on a skirmish line in 1904. (FHFLC.)

Marching, marching, drill, drill, Company C, 2nd Infantry, holds a demonstration on the parade ground in 1905. The company is dressed in khaki uniforms, which were more typical after the Spanish-American War. (FHFLC.)

Col. Francis A. Mansfield, commanding officer of the 2nd Infantry, shown mounted on his horse in this photograph, is identified with an X. Mansfield led the 2nd from March 1904 through January 1906. Colonel Mansfield and his staff appear to be on maneuvers. (FHFLC.)

In 1904–1905, the 2nd Infantry extensively used a target range near Golden, Colorado. Amply documented by William Bevington's photographs, this overhead view shows Companies M, L, K, and I on maneuvers at that location. They are housed in tents with a large mess tent and one labeled chapel and library. (FHFLC.)

Troops of the 2nd Infantry, M Company, with ready mess gear, stand in a line waiting for food service during a 1904 Golden target range camp. (FHFLC.)

A Fort Logan infantry company, camped at the target range near the foothills, forms a meal line. (FHFLC.)

Soldiers of the 2nd Infantry on 1904 maneuvers sit on the ground to eat after being served by the field kitchen. In this William Bevington photograph, they are located at the Golden target range. (FHFLC.)

These 2nd Infantry, A Company soldiers were photographed by Bevington while finishing dinner at the Golden target range in 1904. (FHFLC.)

Thought to be a photograph by William Bevington, this view shows soldiers on a march, probably near the fort. Perhaps the dog in the center has followed them from camp. (FHFLC.)

In 1905, the Army purchased 960 acres of land for a target range in Douglas County, Colorado. Located about 20 miles south of Fort Logan, it was in a more rural area than Golden. This skirmish line maneuver may have been photographed at that location. (FHFLC.)

Here is another view of the skirmish training on a maneuver site near Fort Logan. Note the outline of the foothills in the distance. (FHFLC.)

In 1908, Congress appropriated $100,000 to purchase an additional 338.4 acres, including water rights, to expand the Fort Logan military reservation. This undated photograph by William Bevington shows soldiers camped near the Loretto Heights Academy Building, which was occupied by the Sisters of Loretto Catholic Order. Fort Logan was redesignated as a recruit depot by General Orders No. 91, War Department, on May 5, 1909. (FHFLC.)

A panoramic photograph of the Fort Logan enlisted barracks includes a view of the nearby bandstand, located adjacent to the wide expanse of the parade ground. (FHFLC.)

GUARD DETAIL, FT. LOGAN, COLO.

This postcard portrays the moment when a guard detail is forming next to a Fort Logan enlisted barracks in the early 1900s. (FHFLC.)

The 19th Band Company of the recruit depot occupied this barracks building during the first decade of the 1900s. This postcard establishes how this barracks was architecturally very different from the other enlisted quarters. It also was located apart from the other groups of barracks buildings. (FHFLC.)

This postcard depicts the 9th Band Company barracks around 1910. Originally, there were six enlisted barracks buildings in this style to the southeast of Officers' Row. With the display of bedding, this was evidently "airing day." (FHFLC.)

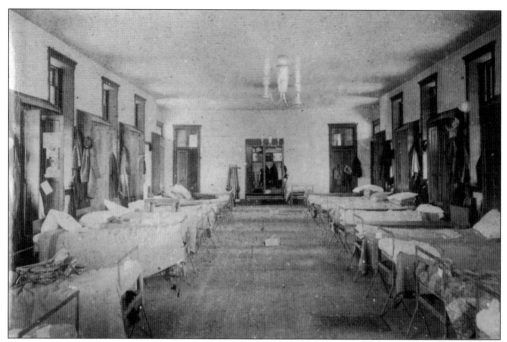

This photograph provides an excellent view of the typical open-bay enlisted barracks with Army cots along the walls. Note the coal oil light fixture in the center of the ceiling. (FHFLC.)

A lone soldier stands in the kitchen of Company G enlisted men's barracks. The room contains only the most essential items and nothing more. (CHS.)

This photograph captures Fort Logan 2nd Infantry troops in their typical open-bay barracks sleeping quarters. The barracks, like this one, were lighted by coal oil lamps until 1904, as indicated in this interior view. (FHFLC.)

A group of seven soldiers relaxes informally with two dogs. These young men, single and far from home, always enjoyed the companionship of pets. (FHFLC.)

In infantry training, drilling and going on maneuvers were the norm. To avoid "all work and no play makes Jack a dull boy," these Company M, 2nd Infantry, soldiers were caught by photographer Bevington allegedly "celebrating one's birthday." Note the standard Army cots of the time. (FHFLC.)

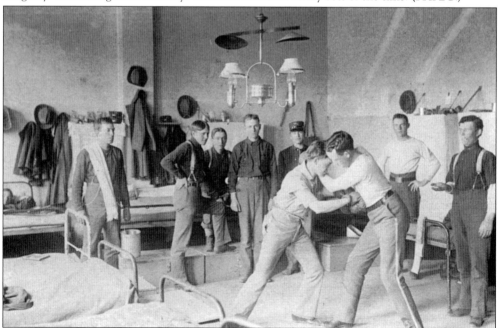

Whether formal boxing matches, or informal athletics, several photographs of men boxing at Fort Logan have survived from 1904. This one shows two men in F Company, 2nd Infantry, in their barracks with seven onlookers. (FHFLC.)

Another photograph depicts boxing outside an enlisted barracks. Five men in marching or guard detail uniforms watch the match. One suspects this was deliberately posed for the photographer. (FHFLC.)

Officers oversee and judge a formal track competition. In this race, there are a number of lanes but only one clear winner dressed in white athletic clothes. The absence of civilians indicates this may have been a competition between different Army units. (FHFLC.)

Fort Logan track and field events were held for various military units and athletes from nearby communities. In this photograph, men are competing in the shot put. (FHFLC.)

These four silver trophies were given for field day athletic events at Fort Logan. Competitors from communities, such as Littleton, would be invited to participate in some meets. (FHFLC.)

A group of 2nd Infantry noncommissioned officers (sergeants) are pictured by a Fort Logan building. (FHFLC.)

DRESS PARADE, FORT LOGAN.   Bevington, Photo.

Troops form for a dress parade in this c. 1905 postcard, which is attributed to William Bevington. Bevington photographs from 1902 to 1909 constitute most of the documentation of Fort Logan during this period. A crowd of onlookers, enjoying the ceremony, can be seen to the right. (FHFLC.)

Company L of the 2nd Infantry is photographed in a parade in downtown Denver in 1904 as part of the celebration in hosting the Grand Army of the Republic (GAR) Convention. GAR, an organization of Civil War Union veterans, was commanded in its early years by Gen. John A. Logan, the Civil War general for whom Fort Logan was named. Note the streetcar behind the marching troops. (FHFLC.)

The two-story Fort Logan Post Exchange Building is shown in this postcard. On this card, a soldier wrote to his mother saying, "Here are a few of the buildings of Fort Logan. We are leaving this p.m. for San Francisco, California, we didn't know till noon where we were going." Note the early-1900s-era car parked in front and the tents in the background. (FHFLC.)

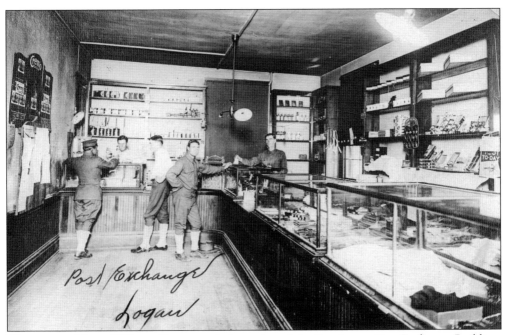

This postcard from 1912 provides a rare indoor view of the Fort Logan Post Exchange Building. All manner of personal supplies were sold to soldiers, but no liquor. (FHFLC.)

Before World War I, post activities included theater events in the YMCA Building. Note the vintage automobile. (FHFLC.)

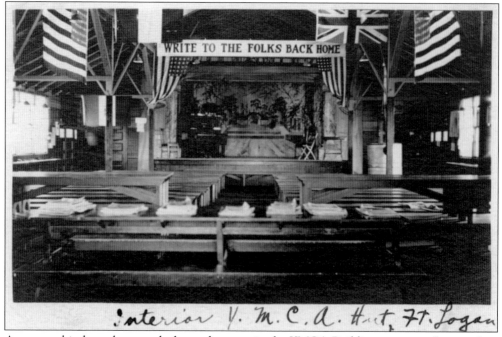

Interior Y. M. C. A. Hut, Ft. Logan

An unusual indoor photograph shows the stage in the YMCA Building, patriotic flags, and an eternal refrain for all soldiers, "Write to the Folks Back Home." (FHFLC.)

Fifth Recruit Company

Fort Logan, Colorado.

A dance program from October 12, 1911, was a souvenir of the Grand Ball held by the 5th Band Company of the recruit depot. Dances listed included the two-step, waltzes, and a grand march. (FHFLC.)

A "reveille gun," sometimes called a "salute gun," originally used in the Civil War, was intended to rouse men for morning activities. The Fort Logan gun has been moved numerous times and is now located in front of the Field Officers' Quarters, the present-day museum of the Friends of Historic Fort Logan. Numerous tents can be seen in the background. (FHFLC.)

By the beginning of World War I, tents filled the Fort Logan landscape. They both housed the men and were used in off-post maneuvers. Recruits were subject to the draft and came from many towns and villages. Local newspapers of the day published accounts of the first day of recruit activities—medical examinations, vaccinations, issuing shoes and uniforms, and endless paperwork. (DPL.)

This postcard depicts stacked rifles and equipment placed before cone-like tents at a World War I recruit camp. (FHFLC.)

Another World War I–era postcard shows Fort Logan troops in formation before beginning guard duty at their tent camp. The mess tent and rugged outdoor tables and benches can be seen on the right. (FHFLC.)

In this postcard, some soldiers cross the parade ground in front of the guardhouse and the "Examining and Receiving Barracks." Note the very tall flagpole; reportedly, it came from a Navy ship. It naturally was always a landmark and remains so today at Fort Logan. (FHFLC.)

During the mobilization for World War I, Fort Logan primarily served as a reception center for recruits. In this photograph by George L. Beam, new recruits in civilian clothes leave a train near the fort's quartermaster's building. (FHFLC.)

After the train arrival at Fort Logan, World War I civilian-clothed recruits march across the parade ground headed for the barracks buildings. A small group of spectators, probably military dependents, sit on the lawn watching the procession of new men. (FHFLC.)

In this George L. Beam photograph, unidentified soldiers lead the recruits, toting bags, to the enlisted barracks at Fort Logan. The corner of the barracks is in view on the left. (FHFLC.)

91488-INSPECTION OF RECRUITS, FORT LOGAN, COLO.

This postcard depicts World War I recruits standing for inspection near several of the enlisted barracks. (FHFLC.)

91486-"WAR BREAD," FORT LOGAN, COLORADO.

A Fort Logan central bakery prepared many loaves of bread daily, which were then distributed to unit messes in the barracks or to troops in the field. This postcard labeled the loaves as "war bread." (FHFLC.)

One destination for the "war bread" in the preceding postcard could have been the tables of this mess hall, which are obviously set for a forthcoming meal. Enlisted mess halls were usually located on the first level of the barracks. The Spartan room and furnishings did not prove conducive to lingering discussions after meals. (FHFLC.)

One of the first tasks for new men coming into the Army was to procure their uniforms and equipment. This process at the Fort Logan quartermaster's building was captured in a photograph during World War I. (FHFLC.)

The quartermaster's building served as a supply store and delivery area for Army material of all sorts. As illustrated in this scene from the World War I era, both cars and wagons were still in use. (FHFLC.)

91487-RECRUITS DEPARTING FOR OTHER POSTS

After enlistment processing and very basic training, troops would form long lines, as seen here, to march to the Fort Logan railroad spur in order to be transported to other posts. (FHFLC.)

This postcard shows Fort Logan World War I soldiers approaching a troop train for transport to other Army posts for continued training. (FHFLC.)

After processing into the US Army at Fort Logan in World War I, soldiers would then be assigned to other installations for training in various specialties, such as artillery. These troops appear to be preparing to board the train. (FHFLC.)

Photographer George L. Beam superbly recorded a telling moment at Fort Logan. Having been processed, soldiers received their World War I uniforms and equipment, then prepared to board a train for further war training. Note the haversacks slung over the mens' shoulders. (FHFLC.)

In May 1918, Col. D.L. Howell, Fort Logan commanding officer, announced that since September over 18,500 soldiers had transited the fort. One of those 18,500 men, this unidentified soldier was a member of the 5th Recruit Company. He had his portrait made in the typical Army uniform of the World War I period. (FHFLC.)

To help the World War I soldiers, a community war council was formed locally. Newspaper accounts described the council's acquisition of a phonograph, a billiard table, player piano rolls, and other entertainment devices. The organization also promoted a 10¢ fare from Fort Logan to the Denver trolley line. Allegedly, jitney drivers had been gouging the troops with a 25¢ charge. Since a soldier's pay was roughly $1 a day, making the trip to downtown proved too expensive for many. This photograph displays one of the modes of transportation that was used at the time. (FHFLC.)

Three

BETWEEN THE
WORLD WARS

This c. 1930 winter photograph shows the Fort Logan headquarters (right), the 110-foot flagpole flying the American flag, and the guardhouse (center). During the period between the world wars, Fort Logan initially continued as a recruit depot. In February 1922, however, the recruit depot was discontinued. In the remainder of the interwar years, the main Army occupant was the 2nd Engineer Battalion, which did rehabilitation work on fort facilities while conducting its normal Army engineer training. In the 1920s, Fort Logan provided facilities for the Citizens' Military Training Camps (CMTC) during that program's summer courses. With the onset of the Great Depression, other organizations such as the Civilian Conservation Corps (CCC) and a reserve officers' training program were active at Fort Logan. (FHFLC.)

Shown early in the 1920s, recruits are marching on the parade ground in the winter wearing long military overcoats. A recruit has placed an "X" over one barracks, evidently marking the quarters where he was likely housed. Note the bleak look of a Colorado winter. (FHFLC.)

Three troops of the recruit depot can be seen lounging under trees on the parade ground. In the background are barracks, and to the right is a cannon. Vintage cars are seen on the drive located around the parade ground. (FHFLC.)

Fort Logan troops, still using mule trains for transportation, embark on military maneuvers in the Colorado mountains in the early 1900s. (FHFLC.)

A Fort Logan soldier has been photographed on his horse. At the time this picture was taken in the early 1920s, the Army was still dependent on horses. Cavalry units were stationed at Fort Logan periodically beginning in 1894. (FHFLC.)

The Dwight D. Eisenhower family lived at Fort Logan in the right section of this Officers' Row duplex from December 1924 to September 1925. Most junior officers with a family lived in duplexes. Single-family houses were provided for the commanding officer and for field officers (for rank of major or higher). (FHFLC.)

Mamie Dowd Eisenhower is pictured with son John in this 1925 portrait. Her husband, Maj. Dwight Eisenhower, had been transferred from the infantry to the Adjutant General (AG) Corps and sent to Fort Logan for brief recruiting duty. The Eisenhowers resided in a duplex next to the current Fort Logan Museum. (CMHI-FL.)

SECOND ENGINEERS FORT LOGAN, COLO. – WAR STRENGTH CO. WITH NEW MOTOR EQUIPMENT

The new, modern, inter–world wars motor equipment is displayed in this photograph with the 2nd Engineer War Strength Company standing at attention in front of their vehicles. However, four officers are shown mounted on horses, and mule teams can be seen ready to transport supplies. (FHFLC.)

The 2nd Engineer men are captured in this photograph setting up camp on maneuvers in the Colorado Springs area. The scenic 14,110-foot Pikes Peak looms in the background. (FHFLC.)

The 2nd Engineer soldiers have pitched tents and stand ready for an inspection on the Fort Logan parade ground. The 2nd Engineer unit had arrived from Fort Sam Houston in 1927. (FHFLC.)

The 2nd Engineer Battalion had begun transitioning to motor vehicles, but in this photograph, the soldiers were still using the Fort Logan stables and other buildings nearby. Barracks buildings can be noted in the background. (FHFLC.)

In this 1936 photograph, a convoy of 6-by-6 trucks belonging to the 2nd Engineer Battalion has stopped on a road on maneuvers into the foothills. These trucks would be used extensively in World War II. (FHFLC.)

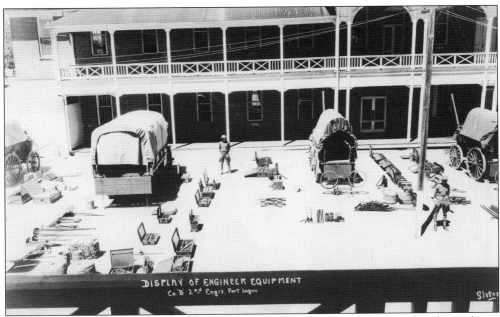

DISPLAY OF ENGINEER EQUIPMENT
Co. B 2ⁿᵈ Engrs. Fort Logan

The engineers are shown preparing a display of engineering equipment at a time when horse-drawn wagons are being replaced by motor vehicles. The arrayed equipment constitutes an interesting mix of picks, shovels, engineering gear, bicycles, heavy jacks, rope, shotguns, and machine guns. (FHFLC.)

Erection of Trestle Bridge by 2nd Engineers, 5/25/34. Sluter

This action photograph shows members of the 2nd Engineers at work lowering a bridge support with the help of a vintage crane. The rear wheels of the crane have a tank-like track for better traction and stability. The solid rubber front tires indicate an old vehicle, possibly built in the early 1920s. (FHFLC.)

Trestle bent bridge erected for General Inspector at Fort Logan, 6-9-34
Time: 1 hr. 17 min.

This 1934 photograph indicates the engineer-built bridge has been completed and is now ready for inspection. The 2nd Engineer Battalion had a mission to move troops and equipment over all kinds of barriers while men were advancing in a military campaign. Note the time on the photograph states it was probably finished in one hour and seventeen minutes. Speed in construction time always assumed far greater importance in wartime, and thus was emphasized in engineer training. (FHFLC.)

This 1928 photograph shows one of the 2nd Engineer Battalion's baseball teams. Participation in team sports was encouraged for fitness, camaraderie, and team building. (FHFLC.)

Team sports were popular activities at Fort Logan. A spirited football game, played between Headquarters Service Company and the 2nd Engineer Battalion, was captured in this 1930 photograph. The score was an exciting 0-0. Note the helmets and lack of pads. FHFLC.)

econd U.S. Engineers on parade in Denver, Sept. 7 1934

The 2nd Engineer's band, troops, and vehicles are on parade in downtown Denver in 1934. The large S.H. Kress & Co. store is prominent in the background, and the sign of the familiar May Company can be seen in the upper right-hand corner. (FHFLC.)

The 2nd Engineer Battalion used these Fort Logan stables and barracks while quartered at the post beginning in 1927. The unit had a long history dating back to the Civil War. They were most welcomed at the fort as they worked on rehabilitation of some facilities. (FHFLC.)

This aerial photograph shows the scope of the military area of Fort Logan in the early 1930s. Many of the buildings have survived but are in far different use today. (FHFLC.)

During the interwar period, the train connections with Denver and other communities were very important for military movements and morale trips for Fort Logan personnel. The Denver, South Park & Pacific had laid track west of Denver and built a small depot halfway between Denver and Morrison. This small station received a "Fort Logan" sign as the fort was constructed in 1888–1889. Note the long outdoor bench. (FHFLC.)

DEPOT, FORT LOGAN, COLO.

The most important rail connection to Denver was the Denver & Rio Grande Railroad with its major, picturesque Fort Logan station. The commuter-type train, called the "Uncle Sam," ran from Denver to Fort Logan and to Littleton and other communities several times daily. This postcard captures the arrival of a train and a mule team nearby. (FHFLC.)

Denver and Rio Grande R. R.

TIME CARD SUBURBAN TRAINS

IN EFFECT JULY 1, 1902.

BETWEEN

DENVER

AND

OVERLAND PARK,
PETERSBURG,
MILITARY PARK,
FORT LOGAN,
LITTLETON.

FOR COMMUTATION RATES SEE LAST PAGE.

S. K. HOOPER, GEN'L PASS. AND TICKET AGENT,
DENVER. COLO.

This railroad advertisement promotes rail service beginning in 1902, but it basically continued throughout all the interwar years. The Denver & Rio Grande service to Fort Logan, called the "Uncle Sam" by Loganites and others, proved to be a very important transportation link for a very long time. (FHFLC.)

Citizens' Military Training Camps were conducted at Fort Logan starting in 1921. Under the National Defense Act, the War Department was charged with providing military training for young men. Each summer, 30 courses were held. This photograph shows a group of trainees and the tents that housed them at the gate to the training area. (FHFLC.)

FORT LOGAN, COLORADO · 1930

CMTC

GET IN TOUCH WITH~

STATE HEADQUARTERS   OR _____
515 Kittredge Bldg.   Denver, Colorado
    Telephone KEystone 5159

This poster was used to recruit 17- to 24-year-old men for the CMTC program. The basic course occurred the first summer and the more advanced Red, White, and Blue Courses followed in the second, third, and fourth summers. (FHFLC.)

83

Summer trainees are shown on the firing line at the rifle range in 1924. The CMTC provided training in weapons of different Army branches, such as infantry, cavalry, field artillery, and coast artillery. (FHFLC.)

On August 10, 1923, a battalion of CMTC recruits marched in the large civic and military parade in Denver to solemnize the burial of President Harding. Recruits fired a cannon as a memorial salute to Harding. The cannon, pictured here, is now in front of the Field Officers' Quarters, which is home to the Friends of Historic Fort Logan Museum. (FHFLC.)

CMTC camper Alfred D. Kleyhauer practices firing a Browning .30–06 machine gun at Fort Logan in a 1930 summer program. The man beside him is one of the World War I regular Army veterans in charge of training and maneuvers. In the background are wagons and old cars. (FHFLC.)

Drum major Eugene Ferrand, a fourth-year student at the CMTC, stands at attention in front of the band. (FHFLC.)

The Citizens' Military Training Camp band entertained at the July 4, 1932, patriotic exercises at Fort Logan. Reportedly, one inducement for being in the band was being excused from kitchen police (KP) duty. (FHFLC.)

These young members of the CMTC band provided dance music for the Officers' Ball in July 1927 because there was no other funding available to hire musicians. Note the colorful painted backdrop behind the band. (FHFLC.)

During the Great Depression years, a New Deal program, called the Civilian Conservation Corps (CCC), occupied buildings at Fort Logan. Jobless young men were put to work on numerous civic projects throughout the nation. Pictured is a 48-man capacity CCC barracks that was completed at Fort Logan in 1935 for a cost of $1,356.65. The CCC also had a headquarters on the post at one time. (FHFLC.)

In May 1933, the Fort Logan commander was asked to administer the units of the CCC in Colorado. Various work projects were planned, and work camps were established near the project sites. This snapshot shows a CCC campsite near Morrison, Colorado. Mount Morrison can be seen in the background with tents and vehicles in front. (FHFLC.)

The majority of the Colorado Depression-era CCC camps in the summer of 1933 were located at altitudes from 7,500 to 10,000 feet. One such site, often termed "at the end of the road," was this one at Estes Park (7,522 feet). CCC men would deploy to the many work projects from Fort Logan. (FHFLC.)

During the 1930s, a significant building project began to provide better quarters for Fort Logan noncommissioned officers (NCO). A number of NCO quarters, like this one, were built on the eastern side of the fort. Building No. 122, the duplex shown here, was constructed in 1933 at a cost of $6,496 and included a Servel electric refrigerator and a gas range. Most of these attractive buildings still exist today. (FHFLC.)

Four

WORLD WAR II
AND BEYOND

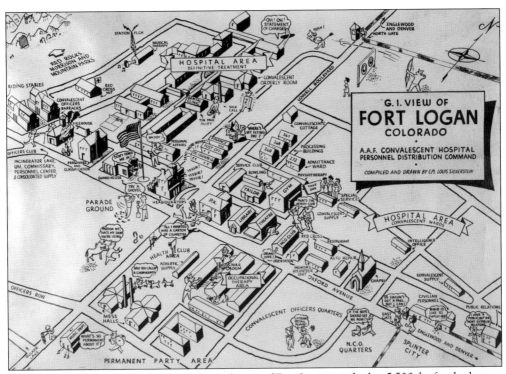

During World War II (1941–1945), the population of Fort Logan peaked at 5,500, by far the largest number ever based at the post. The war mobilization required many new buildings, but most were temporary wooden structures. A c. 1944 "G.I. view of Fort Logan," compiled and drawn by Cpl. Louis Silverstein, humorously depicted some of the many activities at the wartime Fort, among them the Army Air Forces' convalescent hospital. Besides that major function, the post served as a training base, a separation and discharge center between 1945 and 1946, and after the war a Veterans Administration hospital. (FHFLC.)

This June 1940 convoy of vehicles of the 18th Engineer Brigade illustrates the military movements around the country as preparations for World War II building projects began. Most of Fort Logan's expansions had been accomplished before December 1941. (DPL.)

When the Army Air Corps decided in 1941 to use Fort Logan facilities as a training sub-post to Lowry Field, temporary structures were added to the stock of older and more substantial buildings. Many airmen and soldiers were housed throughout World War II in wooden barracks like this one. Note the new water tank that has appeared on post. (FHFLC.)

On February 1, 1941, with the surge in military mobilization leading to World War II, the Army Air Corps at Lowry Field in Denver established a sub-post at Fort Logan to train clerical personnel. Class 9-41TC of the 22nd School Squadron at Fort Logan was photographed at their graduation on June 20, 1941. (Courtesy of Wings Over the Rockies Museum/Photo Archives.)

An administrative inspectors' school became part of the Lowry Field sub-post in June 1942 when it was moved from Knollwood Field in North Carolina. The instructors, pictured here, taught both military and civilian clerks the methods and procedures for issuing combat orders. (FHFLC.)

3705AB. 9 JAN.'45, 2000, WAC TYPING CLASS

The Army Air Corps sub-post at Fort Logan began clerical instruction on March 3, 1941. Classes, like this one of a Women's Army Corps (WAC) typing training, continued at Fort Logan until the end of the war in 1945. (Courtesy of Wings Over the Rockies Museum/Photo Archives.)

Fort Logan NCO Club

Free time was scarce at Fort Logan during World War II, but the noncommissioned officers' club offered an informal gathering place. Lt. A.D. Way (wearing the Army Air Forces flight cap) posed for this photograph while visiting the NCO bar. (FHFLC.)

The Army Air Forces Tactical Training Command (AAFTTC), while operating at Fort Logan, sponsored many theatrical and musical events at the post theater. Built in 1933 for $20,000, the theater measured 50 feet by 100 feet, including the marquee and auditorium with stage. (FHFLC.)

The 1944 Fort Logan "Theater Men" pose in front of the post theater building. They were responsible for arranging, and perhaps performing, the entertainment, including musical programs, theatrical performances, and other events. Note the typical World War II summer uniforms. (FHFLC.)

Troops at Fort Logan exercise under the Colorado spring sunshine, led by their physical fitness instructors. The Rocky Mountain foothills are visible in the background. (FHFLC.)

Fort Logan's obstacle course was famous, or infamous, according to some. The course was designed and laid out by the physical fitness staff. They are shown leading men through it around 1943. (FHFLC.)

A Fort Logan physical fitness instructor encourages trainees to make the leap off the platform in the obstacle course. This obstacle proved tough on feet and ankles. (FHFLC.)

NORTON FAMOUS FOR HIS QUOTES:
"IF YOUSE THINK YOUSE BEAT - YOUSE BEAT"
" YOUSE GUYS CAN DO IT - ITS A JOKE"

EASIER WHEN YOU MAKE IT

Fort Logan trainees wore an interesting array of clothing at this obstacle. Apparently, some expected to land in the water, while others did not. (FHFLC.)

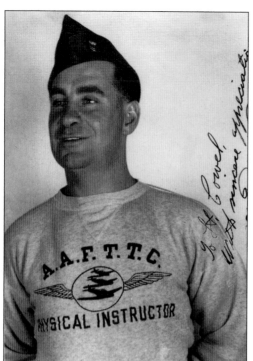

One of the more notable Fort Logan physical instructors was Lt. B.C. "Bo" Cowell, who wrote a conditioning manual for the Army Air Forces personnel. He contributed many of the photographs of fitness training at the post. After discharge in 1946, he joined the athletic staff at Colorado A&M in Fort Collins (now called Colorado State University). (Courtesy of Kent Cowell.)

The sprinting program was an important part of conditioning at Fort Logan during World War II. An instructor points out the proper form for a quick start. (FHFLC.)

LT TRACTOR EXERCISES THE NURSES

Fitness exercises included the nurses. Here, Lieutenant Tractor leads a group in conditioning routines. This exercise was likely conducted in the post gymnasium. (FHFLC.)

During World War II, Fort Logan personnel were given one period weekly for games. In this photograph, touch football was underway on the barren training grounds with the Rocky Mountain Front Range in the background. (FHFLC.)

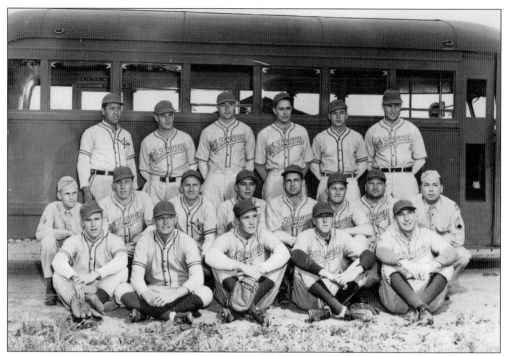

Fort Logan sponsored a variety of sports teams, including this c. 1943 baseball team. Busses, like the one behind the team, transported the players to other cities and other military installations. These teams boosted morale and promoted good relations with local communities. (FHFLC.)

The World War II Fort Logan basketball team, pictured here, played against Buckley Field, Lowry Field, Fort Warren (Wyoming), Fitzsimmons Hospital, 8th Air Force Headquarters, Regis College, and Colorado A&M. (FHFLC.)

Approximately 500 bands served in the Army during World War II. Bands were organized into three types, special, separate, and organization. Separate bands, such as this 27-man band pictured at Fort Logan, supported the administrative, technical, and training centers to which they were attached. Bands often performed at Red Cross and USO dances and played concerts for civilians in addition to their other duties at the post. (FHFLC.)

Leaders were trained at the Army Music School to direct bands like the 6th Army Air Force's band, shown here at Fort Logan in April 1943. Capt. Glenn Miller, the most recognized big-band name, was director of band training for the entire AAFTTC, of which Fort Logan was a part. (FHFLC.)

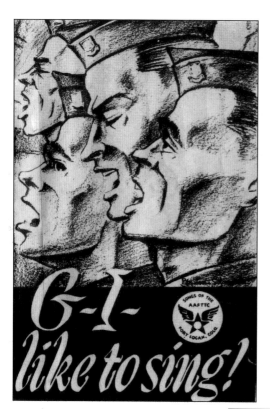

The Special Services and Morale Singing Offices at Fort Logan produced this songbook, entitled *G-I-like to sing!* in 1943 as part of the morale singing program of the Army Air Forces Technical School. (FHFLC.)

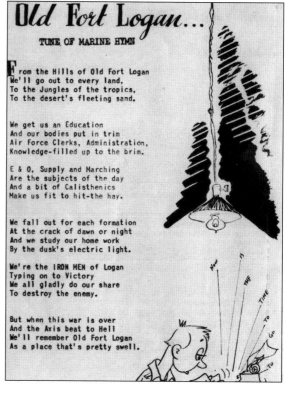

"Old Fort Logan," sung to the tune of the "Marine Hymn," was perhaps a favorite of Maj. Gen. John Curry, the commanding officer at the AAFTTC 4th District Headquarters. He was known to congratulate the officers and men for their "fine singing." (FHFLC.)

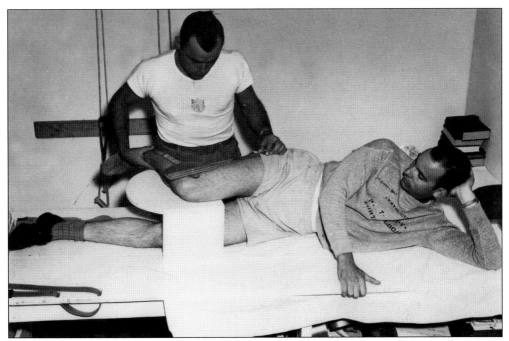

An important activity at Fort Logan during World War II was the rehabilitation of injured men. In this photograph, a likely trainee measures the leg and knee joint of a Fort Logan physical therapy instructor. (FHFLC.)

STAFF ENLARGED FOR REHABILATION HOSPITAL
PARRISH -TOWNER-CLEARY-GIBSON-COY- VIDAKAVICH~SCHNEIDER-WHITE-WILHELM-PORRETTA
LT. HANSMA - LT COWEL-CAPT WARNER- CAPT. NOBLE- LT TRACKTER-LT TEFFERTEILER - LT ANDERSON
BOLTON -ZENOBIA- ABRAMS -FLETCHER-OGDEN - BLATTNER-NAVA-JONES
FREIDMAN- SIMONE-BOLTON-EINHORN-CARMICHAEL-ABERNATHY
SEE BACK SIDE OF PICTURE FOR FIRST NAME-RANK-STATE

Fort Logan's war activities focused not only on training and conditioning but also on physical rehabilitation. The rehabilitation hospital's staff members gathered for this photograph around 1944. Note the two unidentified men in the midst of the white-clad staff members. (FHFLC.)

Staff and possibly patients sit on the steps of a Fort Logan hospital barracks at the end of World War II. The soldier in front holds a white cane, possibly indicating blindness. Another soldier holds a newspaper that reads, "Peace at Last." Fort Logan closed as a military post in 1946. However, the Veterans Administration continued to use the hospital until a new VA hospital was constructed in Denver in 1951. (FHFLC.)

An Army nurse holds an envelope full of paperwork as she stands next to a Fort Logan hospital barracks. (FHFLC.)

Gen. Dwight D. Eisenhower, who once lived on Fort Logan, returned to the post in an inspection on February 17, 1946. In this photograph, Eisenhower speaks to Pvt. James Justice during his separation processing at the Fort Logan Separation Center Barracks. Discharge processing became a very important activity in 1945–1946. (Courtesy of the Eisenhower Presidential Library and Museum, National Archives and Records Administration.)

Gen. Dwight D. Eisenhower, third from the left, chats with Billy Shannon, age eight, son of Col. L.T. Shannon, during a stop at the Fort Logan headquarters on February 17, 1946. (Courtesy of the Eisenhower Presidential Library and Museum, National Archives and Records Administration.)

Many of Fort Logan's structures were repurposed, sold, and removed or demolished between 1946 and 1960, including a large variety of temporary buildings, such as the one shown here. Even the old brick buildings, like the one in the background, did not always escape the wrecking ball. (FHFLC.)

The remains of a concrete structure and a massive chimney, thought to have been the location of the Fort Logan laundry, stand amid the ghostly remnants of other buildings that once housed so many activities. By 1946, the military men had gone as well as most of the buildings. Fortunately, the old historic Officers' Row and the spacious parade ground continued to exist! (FHFLC.)

Five

FORT HOSPITAL TO
MENTAL HEALTH CENTER

POST HOSPITAL—FT. LOGAN.

The Post Hospital was one of the first structures built at Fort Logan. This photograph dates to its earliest days in the late 1880s. Along with many other post buildings, the hospital was designed by civilian architect Frank J. Grodavent. Note the small saplings planted around the building and compare their size with much later pictures. The Post Hospital served a variety of patients until its demolition in the 1950s. (FHFLC.)

This view of the Post Hospital is from a different perspective and a later time. Note the unique hospital architecture and the maturing trees. (FHFLC.)

Diagonally across from the Post Hospital was the Red Cross House for Convalescents at Fort Logan, the large white building that can be seen clearly in this dramatic aerial view looking northwest from the central part of the fort. (FHFLC.)

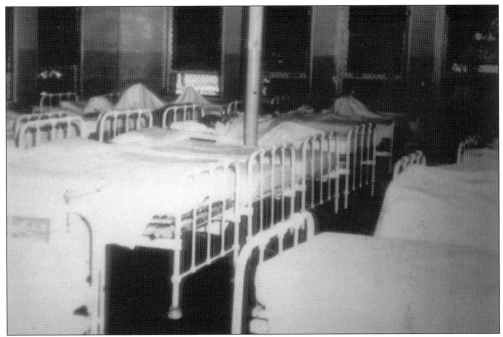

As illustrated here, the older hospital wards of Fort Logan were austere with a notable lack of privacy or personal space. Infection control under these conditions must have been a challenge. Several patients can be seen resting on their beds in this rare interior photograph. (CMHI-FL.)

The Post Hospital is shown here in its last years. The saplings have matured to large shade trees, and an accommodation to the automobile is obvious with the circular drive, which can still be seen today. Over time, some of the fort buildings were neglected and required much repair. Much rehabilitative work occurred in the 1930s. During World War II, the hospital was used extensively by the Army Air Forces as a convalescent facility. (FHFLC.)

The recreation area of the Red Cross House for Convalescents, shown in this photograph, invited relaxation and socialization among the recuperating Army personnel. Note the unusual architectural design of the support beams in the ceiling, which provided an open, airy ambience thought to be conducive to healing. (FHFLC.)

A group of unidentified Fort Logan Medical Department men is pictured in March 1928. The formal photograph was probably taken on the lawn in front of the wide porch of the Post Hospital. (FHFLC.)

The Red Cross House for Convalescents can be seen looking straight north, between the guardhouse to the left and the headquarters building to the right. In the foreground, the 2nd Engineer Battalion and attached reserve officers were deployed on the Fort Logan parade ground, apparently waiting for an inspection. (FHFLC.)

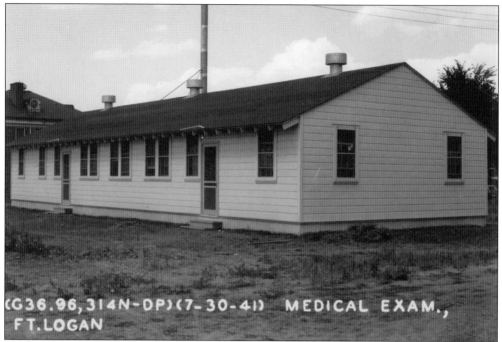

(G36.96, 314N-DP)(7-30-41) MEDICAL EXAM., FT.LOGAN

During World War II, the greatly increased Fort Logan population demanded the expansion of hospital facilities. A number of temporary wooden buildings, such as this 1941 medical examination building, were hastily added. (FHFLC.)

(G36.97, 314N-DP)(7-30-41) HOSP. WARD, FT. LOGAN

This photograph provides a view of a 1941 temporary wooden building designated as a hospital ward. Buildings like this one housed rehabilitation care for the injured in World War II. (FHFLC.)

Ft. Logan, a military post for nearly six decades, is now Veterans Administration hospital. Surplus barracks converted to apartments.

The Veterans Administration used hospital beds at Fort Logan from 1946 to 1951 until completion of the new Denver VA hospital. This aerial view of the fort looks west toward the mountains. During the Veterans Administration time at Fort Logan, the training of social workers in neuropsychiatric treatment began. (FHFLC.)

After the Veterans Administration left Fort Logan, the state of Colorado took over the acreage of the old fort area and established the Fort Logan Mental Health Center in 1961. This 1992 map shows the transition to the current Colorado Mental Health Institute at Fort Logan with mental health activities occupying original post buildings as well as new added structures. (FHFLC.)

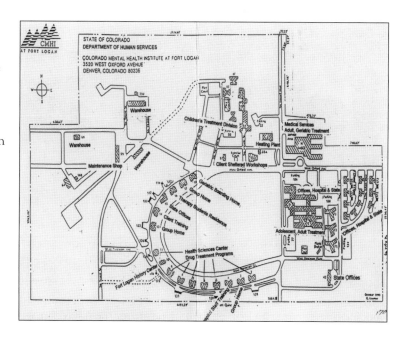

Almost all of Fort Logan's original barracks buildings were demolished in the early 1960s to make way for the construction of the new mental health center. In the far background, only one of the barracks buildings, seen here, survived the demolition. (FHFLC.)

This structure, known as Building No. 42, is the only barracks left standing after the demolition of the other five in the group. Although white in the photograph, it has since been restored to its original brick condition. (FHFLC.)

Some of the people in attendance at the early February 1961 ground breaking ceremony for the Fort Logan Mental Health Center included Gov. Steve McNichols (third from right) and Dr. James Galvin (third from left), director of the Colorado Department of Institutions. (FHFLC.)

This is a photograph of the Arapahoe team at the mental health center shortly before it opened on July 17, 1961. Initially, the center had the following three treatment teams organized according to the surrounding counties that they served: Jefferson, Adams, and Arapahoe. (Courtesy of C. Parker Private collection.)

The Medical-Surgical-Geriatric Building is shown under construction. Along with its patient care units, it housed the pharmacy, laboratory, X-ray department, medical clinic, central medical supply, hospital laundry, and physical therapy, as well as other ancillary services. There were three geriatric units with about 22 beds each. (CMHI-FL.)

This photograph of the completed Medical-Surgical-Geriatric Building in 1964 reflected the open design befitting the new treatment philosophy practiced at Fort Logan. (CMHI-FL.)

This 1960s mental health center complex, seen under construction in the northwest quadrant, housed teams treating children from preteen through age 17 according to their age group. (CMHI-FL.)

The Fort Logan Mental Health Center Administration Building reflected the new idea of openness in psychiatric treatment, which was developed by Dr. Maxwell Jones with his "Therapeutic Community." (FHFLC.)

The chief architect of the new mental health buildings at Fort Logan was Temple Hoyne Buell, who was noted for his unique building designs in Denver. Construction of the first buildings began in early 1961 and included the cottages shown here. They housed treatment teams in modern and spacious facilities. (CMHI-FL.)

One of the major buildings seen at Fort Logan today is the 1960s administration building belonging to the mental health center. The structure reflects the concept of an open, interactive community, a radical departure from the old, traditionally closed, locked designs of psychiatric hospitals. Thus, currently at Fort Logan, a visitor finds a mix of the old military fort and the new approach to mental health treatment. This represents a long evolving journey from Post Hospital to mental health institute. (CMHI-FL.)

Six

FORT CEMETERY TO NATIONAL CEMETERY

"The Bivouac of the Dead" by Theodore O'Hara

The muffled drum's sad toll has beat
The soldier's last tattoo;
No more on Life's parade shall meet
That brave and fallen few.
On Fame's eternal camping-ground
Their silent tents are spread,
And Glory guards, with solemn round,
The bivouac of the dead.

(Courtesy of Fort Logan National Cemetery.)

The cemetery at Fort Logan began in 1889 when land (a little over three acres) near the northwest corner of the post was set aside for a cemetery. The first recorded burial was Mable Peterkin, daughter of Private Peterkin, who died on June 28, 1889. Private Peterkin served with Company E of the 18th Infantry, the very first unit at Fort Logan. (Courtesy of William Leeper.)

The 25th Infantry, an African American regiment, was stationed at Fort Logan from October 1898 to September 1900, and several members of that regiment were buried at the post cemetery. Although Plains Indians were the first to call African American cavalry units "buffalo soldiers," by 1900, newspapers had come to use the term for any black soldier. (Courtesy of National Archives.)

Pvt. James Yancy, a member of the African American Company M, 25th Infantry, was buried at the post cemetery on May 1, 1899. Today, he is remembered as a buffalo soldier. (Courtesy of William Leeper.)

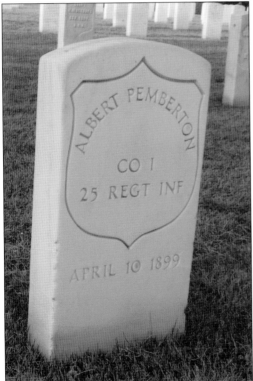

Another buffalo soldier, Pvt. Albert Pemberton, Company I of the African American 25th Infantry, served at Fort Logan until his death on April 10, 1899, and was then interred in the post cemetery. (Courtesy of William Leeper.)

This aerial view of the Fort Logan Cemetery in 1953, oriented with west at the top, shows some street construction and grading taking place as the post cemetery transitions to a national cemetery. The original post burial area is to the right where trees provided a shaded section. Note Sheridan

NATIONAL CEMETERY
FORT LOGAN COLO.
AF 67-2-53

Boulevard separates the cemetery from the developing Bear Valley subdivision. (Courtesy of Fort Logan National Cemetery.)

The National Cemetery System was established by Congress and approved by Pres. Abraham Lincoln in 1862 in order to provide for the proper burial and registration of graves of Civil War veterans. It was not until March 10, 1950, however, that the post cemetery became the Fort Logan National Cemetery. This photograph shows the current impressive main gate. (Courtesy of William Leeper.)

In 1973, the Veterans Administration assumed responsibility for Fort Logan National Cemetery. This photograph shows the seal on a cemetery gate. (Courtesy of William Leeper.)

An unusual 1943 burial at Fort Logan National Cemetery is that of Karl Baatz, a German prisoner of war in World War II. Fort Logan briefly had a prisoner of war camp during the war. At that time, there was still a post cemetery. (Courtesy of William Leeper.)

A number of Medal of Honor veterans have been buried at the cemetery. This gravestone is in memory of Army private John Davis of the Civil War who died in 1901. (Courtesy of William Leeper.)

FRED F HOLCOMBE JR CPL
BENNIE R JESTIS PVT
ROBERT D LaDUKE PVT
DONALD R MYRICK PFC

US MARINE CORPS
FEBRUARY 17 1956

Fort Logan National Cemetery has seven group burials, with the greatest number interred in one grave being eight. The Marine Corps victims of a May 30, 1945, plane crash were not buried until July 1957 after discovery of their lost plane. (Courtesy of William Leeper.)

Out of respect for all persons buried at the Fort Logan National Cemetery, and to indicate mourning, the main flag is lowered to half-staff 30 minutes before the first service and it remains at half-staff until 30 minutes following the last service of the day. (Courtesy of William Leeper.)

Today, Fort Logan National Cemetery has the unique Memorial Path, which provides a serene setting overlooking Memorial Lake. Veterans' organizations have contributed approximately 20 memorial plaques that line the path. (Courtesy of William Leeper.)

Among the memorial plaques is one honoring veterans of the World War II 10th Mountain Division who are buried at the cemetery. The Army 10th Mountain Division has always had a special association with Colorado. (Courtesy of William Leeper.)

Burials of World War II veterans increasingly occupy large areas of the cemetery. More gravestones of Korean War and Vietnam War participants can now be found. Representative of a Vietnam War burial is that of Medal of Honor recipient Army major William E. Adams of the A/227th Assault Helicopter Company, 52nd Aviation Battalion, 1st Aviation Brigade, Kontum Province, Republic of Vietnam. He died in heroic action on May 25, 1971. (Courtesy of William Leeper.)

Civil War general John Alexander Logan began the practice of decorating veterans' graves, which later became known as Memorial Day. Pictured is a Memorial Day observance at the Fort Logan National Cemetery, a fitting reminder of General Logan, whose name was given originally to the old military fort and then to the national cemetery. General Logan's efforts to memorialize the nation's veterans continue today. (Courtesy of Fort Logan National Cemetery.)

BIBLIOGRAPHY

Arps, Louisa Ward. *Denver in Slices*. Athens, OH: Swallow, 1983.

Catlett, Sharon R. *Farmlands, Forts, and Country Life: The Story of Southwest Denver*. Boulder, CO: Big Earth Publishing, 2007.

Dorsett, Lyle W. and Michael McCarthy. *The Queen City: A History of Denver*. Boulder, CO: Pruett Publishing Co., 1986.

"From Infantry to Air Corps: The History of Fort Logan." *Denver Westerners Roundup*. November–December 1986: 3–13.

McChristian, Douglas C. *The US Army in the West, 1870–1880: Uniforms, Weapons and Equipment*. Norman, OK: University of Oklahoma Press, 2006.

McCoy, Earl. "Adventures of Ivy Baldwin, Aerialist." *Denver Westerners Roundup*. March–April 1993: 3–12.

Merriam, Cyrus L. *Captain John Macpherson of Philadelphia*. Brattleboro, VT: Griswold, 1966.

Pfanner, Robert. "Highlights in the History of Fort Logan." *Colorado Magazine*. May 1942: 81–91.

"The Genesis of Fort Logan." *Colorado Magazine*. March 1942: 43–50.

DISCOVER THOUSANDS OF LOCAL HISTORY BOOKS FEATURING MILLIONS OF VINTAGE IMAGES

Arcadia Publishing, the leading local history publisher in the United States, is committed to making history accessible and meaningful through publishing books that celebrate and preserve the heritage of America's people and places.

Find more books like this at
www.arcadiapublishing.com

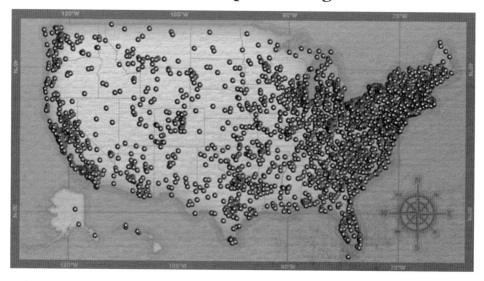

Search for your hometown history, your old stomping grounds, and even your favorite sports team.